About My Hair
A Journey to Recovery

Photographs and Narrative

by

Marcia Reid Marsted

Capelli d'Angeli Press

Canton, Connecticut

About My Hair :
A Journey to Recovery

Copyright © 2001 by **Marcia Reid Marsted**

Library of Congress Control Number: 2002090196

ISBN 0-9716737-0-5

Capelli d'Angeli Press ⁀
125 Indian Hill Road
Canton, Connecticut 06019-3624

www.capellidangelipress.net

First Printing

Printed in Canada

Published in conjunction with the art exhibition
About My Hair :
> **A Journey to Recovery**
>> **The Photographs**
>>> at
The Helen & Harry Gray Cancer Center
Hartford Hospital
Hartford, CT 06102

www.harthosp.org/cancer/welcome.html

For Jeff.

Also for Melissa and Amanda
and their grandmothers,
both of whom died of cancer.

Table of Contents

Preface

First, I am a photographer.

Periodically, I am a cancer patient.

At times I have been a scientist, teacher and biologist.

Always, I am a wife, mother and, now, grandmother.

This is a somewhat haphazard photographic diary

I kept to document changes in my hair.

As I dealt with surgery and a cancer diagnosis,

I learned chemotherapy and hair loss would follow.

I wanted to record my transformations as images

of this new series of events

that were going to change my life.

This book of portraits – of me and my world –

is the result of my decision.

Marcia Reid Marsted, M.A., M.P.H.

This work was funded in part by a Visual Artists Grant from

the Connecticut Commission on the Arts,

by a grant from The Helen and Harry Gray

Cancer Center at Hartford (CT) Hospital

and by a generous donation from Nancy Grover,

a wonderful friend.

About My Hair
A Journey to Recovery

Middle of the Day

White Blooms

Forward

– To confront cancer – "cancer" itself a word that, not very long ago, was not even mentioned aloud by many people, but whispered or abbreviated as if it were a secret vice–is an act of unmitigated bravery. You are brave because you have to be; you are courageous because where there is courage, there is life.

From out of the shadowy wells of courage, many surprises can emerge: understanding, patience, empathy, compassion, awareness, spirituality, humor, connection, love, intimacy – and art. Marcia Reid Marsted's work is a mosaic of all these elements. She embraces the most personal moments, telling us about her responses to her experiences with diagnosis, doctors, the very idea of cancer, survival, and the triumph of the everyday.

Through her use of photography and her spare but dynamic sentences, Marcia shapes her individual experience into a detailed and beautifully honest one; she forges her world into a work of art.

This is not illness as grand opera; it is the quotidian, the familiar, and the simple transformed by the experience of cancer into something else altogether. The clear, clean prose gets to the point, as do the accompanying images.

In some poignant textual moments, Marcia's husband Jeff interjects his own dialogue into the piece. Later on, after the chemo is complete, Jeff writes a response that is haiku-like in quality: "Must be a strange period for all involved with cancer treatment. Anti-climactic is not quite the feeling. Everyone wonders –Now what happens?"

After attending a workshop called *A Gathering of Women Photographers*, Marcia was encouraged by an overwhelming response to use her work to help others undergoing chemotherapy.

The journey has been difficult, but Marcia Reid Marsted has made a thing of beauty from it.

Regina Barreca,
        Professor and Author

Entering the Woods

Introduction

My artistic focus took an unexpected turn

when I discovered I had developed

a second primary cancer,

after ten cancer-free years.

When I realized this chemo would be different,

I began a photographic documentation of myself,

my surroundings, and my relationship to them.

The chemotherapy for uterine cancer

causes total body hair loss.

Hair, or lack of it, is often the most obvious

outward sign of cancer treatment.

I started to keep a journal,

but photographs were the way I wanted

to remember what was happening.

Most of the images in this series

were shot with infrared film.

Infrared film produces an other-worldly look

that was appropriate for me and my response

to undergoing chemotherapy.

In the Mist

On any given day,

I may or may not have felt good,

but I didn't look or feel quite like myself.

My last chemo session was April 27.

In May, still totally hairless,

I attended a photography workshop

called *A Gathering of Women Photographers*.

I brought some of what I called the "hair" photos

for the critique. Until that point,

I hadn't thought about showing them to anyone.

For me, they were my diary.

Everyone suggested I consider

putting the photographs into a book.

I went home with a mission.

If seeing images of me bald could be helpful

to a patient, relative or friend who might be worried

about this unknown

and frightening series of events,

I was willing to expose myself.

My Third Eye

My Third Eye

This picture was an omen.

I was trying to photograph the asymmetries in my face.

Instead, I photographed *My Third Eye*.

That eye was trying to tell me something.

Even then, in 1997, I sensed there was a problem.

I had stopped menstruating

after surgery, radiation and chemotherapy

for rectal cancer in 1988.

Now I was bleeding erratically.

My doctor said it was just

a result of tissue damage from the radiation.

I knew there was more to it.

When Jeff read an early draft and saw the pictures,
he asked if he could write his comments.
I thought they would be a great addition.

Jeff's Thoughts

My first reaction to this photograph was —
is this a printing mistake?
Or is this the real Marcia?
My Gemini: Complex. Beautiful.

Thinking About What Is To Come

I began my photographic journey with this picture.

I took it in early December.

November's surgery scar was healing.

Now it was time to deal with the idea

of heavy-duty chemotherapy and hair loss.

This was going to be a new experience.

Worth documenting, I decided.

It was December. Other people were Christmas shopping.

I was on my way to the hairdresser.

No color and a super-short cut, I decided.

Then, anticipating the baldness to come,

the wig store would be the next stop.

There wouldn't be as much hair to fall out

and I'd be ready for my bald head

with a wig I liked, and had planned for.

This story started a month earlier, with abdominal pain.

Days before an art opening I had yet to hang

was supposed to open, Jeff rushed me to the hospital.

Me Alone

I knew what was happening from past experience.

An intestinal obstruction was blocking my system.

The CT scan to find the obstruction

showed enlargement of my uterus as well.

I wasn't surprised.

I knew the bleeding I'd been experiencing

wasn't due to the radiation.

My surgeon asked me

if I wanted him to arrange for a gynecologist

to remove my uterus and ovaries

after he repaired the obstruction.

I agreed quickly, on the condition that

the surgery wait until after my art opening.

For me it was a relief,

rather than upsetting or sad,

to think that I'd be getting rid of

my bothersome uterus.

The obstruction allowed a little soft food

to pass through my system.

As long as I ate carefully,

a few extra days wouldn't matter that much.

The surgeries were begun at two o'clock in the morning

to fit me into the doctors' busy schedules.

Jeff, sitting, waiting in my hospital room

was aware of how long they took.

I was more or less blissfully asleep.

I recovered quickly

and tried not to worry too much.

It wasn't until the biopsies came back three days later

that we were sure of my diagnosis —

endometrial (uterine) cancer —

that had gone through the wall of my uterus.

Serious enough to require

 adjuvant (additional) treatment.

A Happy Moment

This picture was the second in my series.

I took it just before we walked out the door

heading to the hairdresser and the wig store.

We were on the way to a dramatic moment,

but sitting together for the camera

we could forget it for a while.

When you are sick with cancer,

not every minute is horrible.

Most of the time life goes on

as if everything were normal.

Jeff's Thoughts

A surreal picture of two happy people
enduring their own private hell.
Marcia didn't act or look sick,
which is the evil of cancer.

The Two of Us, Feeling Pretty Good

At the Wig Store

The short haircut didn't look bad.

Next stop, the wig store *.

The shop was very elegant. Pictures of movie stars

and Styrofoam heads covered with wigs

in varying hair colors and styles lined the walls.

The floors were white marble. The mirrored walls

had discreet doors to private consultation booths.

"Do you have an appointment?" the receptionist asked.

My face fell. What made me think I could just walk in

 and pick out a wig like a pair of shoes, and walk out?

The attractive, pleasant man at the desk

told us in a well-modulated, foreign-lilted voice

that he thought he could find a "stylist"

available for a consultation.

Jeff called the insurance company

to see if they would pay for the wig,

dubbed a *medical prosthesis* in insurance-speak.

(* See Appendix: pg 119: "Wigs.")

A Few Curls

I went in to start trying on —

oh, my God! wigs — (whatever the insurance says)

with Edward. He was very gentle.

He asked me questions about my chemo.

I didn't know the answers.

He told me my hair would probably fall out

after the first dose of the drugs, and that my head

was likely to tingle just before it did.

I tried on a wig that was only a little longer

than my spiky butch,

a little more finished-looking,

and about the same shade.

Two more tries: first longer, and then,

an expensive, real-hair model.

Neither was right for me.

The first try was the best.

Edward showed me where the toupee tape

(better known as Scotch) would go

to hold the wig in place when there was no hair.

I began to tremble. I didn't want Jeff to see.

The Short Cut

The New Wig

Edward explained that I'd need two wigs

to last the year of hairlessness.

I would alternate them,

making each one stay fresh longer.

I took one quick photo and then put the wig away.

Soon enough, I would need to wear it.

With a short cut and the new wigs in my closet,

I was prepared for the consequences of the chemo.

Jeff Remembers
It was like my little sister's first haircut.
Then this tragic event became
a glamorous and exotic unveiling,
followed by a fun,
but disturbing
adventure into wigdom.

Ready for Anything

I spent the weekend enjoying my new cut.

The bubble was quickly burst

on Monday morning.

During my post-surgery visit

with my oncologist,

we had an important

and sobering conversation.

"It's extramural," she reminded us.

(Jeff was with me at most office visits.)

The tumor had not been confined

to the inside of my uterus,

but had gone through the uterine wall.

Though it seemed to have been covered

by the loop of bowel

that had caused the obstruction,

there was an increased possibility

that cancer cells had entered my blood vessels

and traveled to other parts of my body.

Chemotherapy was my only choice of therapy.

My treatment for rectal cancer, back in 1988,

had included radiation,

along with surgery and chemo.

Additional radiation

to my remaining abdominal organs

would only serve to damage already delicate tissues.

"We'd better start the chemotherapy

sooner rather than later."

was Pat's suggestion.

No relaxing.

Attack those cancer cells.

My first chemo was scheduled for December 14,

less than a month after my surgery.

Jeff's Thoughts
The cut was not bad. Compared to what?
How soon I forgot.
She is not Marcia.
She's more like a new wife.
Then came the visit with the oncologist.

Reflecting : Short Cut

Reality Sets In

We flew south for a long weekend away from home.

We needed to forget about, as well as prepare for,

the day that was coming all too soon.

I waited until the last minute Monday morning

before getting into the car with Jeff.

We were off to the hospital

for my overnight stay for chemotherapy.

A solicitous nurse hooked me up

to the IV needle and a hydrating drip.

I was almost ready

for my first dose of the chemotherapeutic agents.

Before I could have any chemo,

my oncologist had scheduled

a battery of tests

to make sure my system could

withstand the drugs.

Special tests determined the balance

and levels of the various blood components.

Weighed Down

The <u>MultiGa</u>ted blood-pool imaging test, or MUGA,

examined how well my heart was pumping

and served as a baseline for any future changes.

A repeat of the MUGA near the end of the chemo

would check for changes, including

damage to my heart muscle.

Finally, the nurse weighed me

to determine the precise dose

of all the drugs —

down to the exact milligram

and cubic centimeter.

In the Hospital

Five of my six chemo treatments

took place in the hospital with an overnight stay,

rather than in the cancer center.

In a hospital setting it was easier

for the nurses to make sure

my system was properly hydrated.

The extra fluids helped to prevent

the nausea and vomiting so often associated

with this type of chemo.

A saline solution dripped into my arm

from the moment I arrived in the morning

until just before I left the next day.

For me, a rather solitary person,

the worst aspect of these monthly visits

was the worry about whether I would have a roommate.

Others might worry that there wouldn't be one.

I brought my own pillow and blanket

and a radio, so I could listen to music I liked.

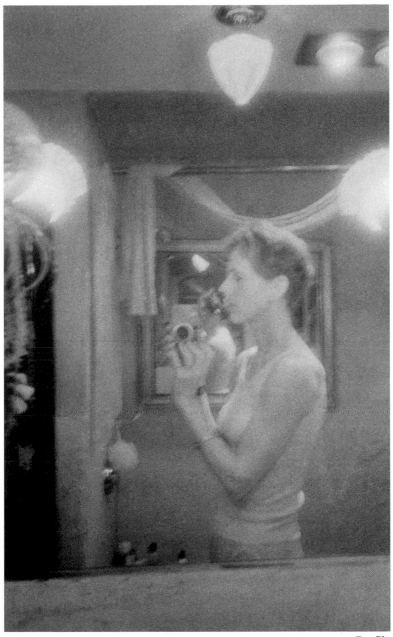

Profile

Special comforts and reminders of home

helped to keep me cheerful.

Family pictures brought everyone into the room.

To insure that I was never bored,

I always brought more

than I would ever have time to do:

my computer, books, magazines, letters to write ....

Each night I would watch thousands of crows

fly over the hospital towards their rookery.

I wondered where they roosted.

I found it beautiful and relaxing

to see them sweeping past me.

Jeff's Memories
We went together to the hospital
for the overnight chemo regimen.
I stayed until 10:00 p.m. or so.
It was very procedural,
not especially medical or informative.
So what, if it works.

Urns in Winter

Watching the Mourning Doves

Everyday Comforts

When I came home from a treatment,

Chatchat, my cat, and I often sat together.

The one-way mirror

in the window feeder in the bedroom

let us watch, unseen,

as the mourning doves

pecked at sunflower seed.

Winter was on the outside,

while we were warm inside.

The View Is Still Quite Normal

The Chemotherapeutic Drugs

Adriamycin and Cisplatin. Killers of fast growing cells.

Killers, then, not only of cancer cells.

but of hair follicles, cells lining the mouth,

and red and white blood cells.

The Adriamycin was a beautiful cherry red.

A nurse injected it from a huge syringe.

She wore gloves and warned me to let her know

if I felt any burning sensations in my arm.

She explained that the drug would make my urine red.

Luckily, she prepared me for that shock.

Cisplatin was a milky white.

It dripped into my vein slowly over an hour or so.

When the Cisplatin bag was empty,

the various anti-nausea drugs were injected or swallowed.

One was a steroid that made my cheeks pink.

They called it the "happy hormone."

I felt a twinge of nausea that first day,

driving to the pharmacy. That was the only time.

After that, those drugs helped me to feel quite normal.

Alternative Therapies

I wanted more guns in my armament.

Acupuncture, Reiki, and the Rosen Method *

put my Yin and Yang back into harmony.

Yoga improved my mental and physical state.

The American Indian, animal-oriented

Medicine Cards I tried to "read" were insightful.

I saw a naturopath and later became

the patient of a homeopathic doctor

recommended by my oncologist.

The homeopath, Molly, suggested two

additional helpful practitioners,

a nutritionist and a psychologist.

Both had a special interest and expertise

in treating cancer patients. Both had survived cancer.

I discovered that massage therapy could be calming,

relaxing and mind-expanding when performed by

the appropriate practitioner.

(* See Appendix pg 120: "Alternative Therapies.")

I didn't make many changes in my eating habits.

My diet was already quite healthy.

I added vitamins and other supplements

suggested by the homeopath and nutritionist,

but I didn't want to give up my daily glass of wine.

In 1989, after my first cancer, I became

an American Cancer Society volunteer.

Once I'd been through a year of treatments

and learned to deal with my own cancer,

I was allowed to help other cancer patients.

I've continued to volunteer.

I believe that thinking of someone besides yourself

can be as therapeutic as drugs.

Jeff's View
Because she has an alternative personality,
and is always curious about anything new or different,
I expected Marcia to explore alternative therapies.
I hope I supported her.
I even joined in at times.
Nothing was silly or frivolous.
I guess that was her way of continuing the fight.

Hair Getting Thinner

The Loss of My Hair

My wigs waited on the closet shelf,

on their Styrofoam heads.

I managed to keep my hair

until after New Year's Eve.

I was very gentle

with both my hair and my head.

I didn't wash or even comb it much.

It stayed looking relatively normal

until after the second dose of chemo

on January 5.

About a week later my hair began to fall out.

The wig was soon to have a coming out.

Looking for a Reason to Smile

As my hair began to lose its hold

on my scalp,

I finally had to wash what was left.

That morning,

as Jeff walked into the bathroom,

I realized how much alike we looked.

I took this picture of us smiling

to give us a smile later on.

Jeff Speaks
I looked worse than Marcia.
Did that have to be recorded?
All is fair in love and sickness.
I didn't laugh at her.

The Two of Us in the Mirror – Looking Similar

Most Difficult Moments

Here are my blessedly short tresses

going down the drain.

I felt pleased with myself

that I'd had the foresight to cut my hair before the chemo,

so that what floated down the tub

was not too depressing.

It was still pretty awful, even with my planning.

Luckily, the disappearance only took

three or four days.

A bald head is a shock.

The disappearance of eyebrows and eyelashes

is not any easier.

Pubic hair disappeared, too.

Every hair was eventually —

gone.

Jeff's Thoughts

The picture was a shock.
Either I don't remember, didn't know or blocked it out.
The hair just left – with the cancer, I hoped.

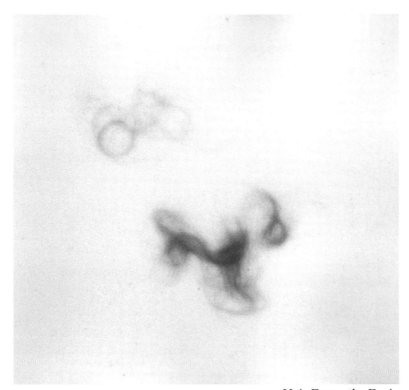

Hair Down the Drain

Unguents

Feminine Beautifiers

Most of these lotions and potions

were useless on my bald body.

I covered my skin with moisturizer

to keep it from drying out.

Sores appeared in my mouth from the chemo.

I had a special mouthwash

and, as the sores got worse,

special prescription swishes.

The best thing about not having any hair

was not having to worry about it.

The daily shampoos, the leg shaving,

and the trips to the hairdresser

were all unnecessary for a while.

Jeff Speaks
There were no haircuts, shampoos, razors,
whatever a woman needs to maintain a look.
There was no hair anywhere.

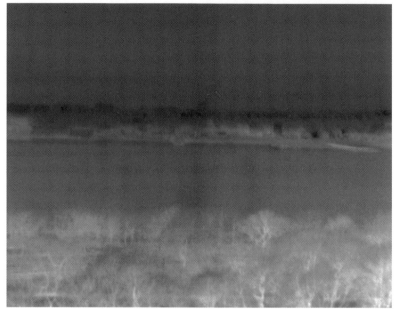

The Long View

Rejuvenation of the Blood

Every other day during the week after a treatment

I gave myself shots of the monoclonal antibodies,

Procrit and Neupogen, that induced my body

to make more red and white blood cells.

Chemotherapeutic agents go after any fast-growing cells.

Like cancer cells, blood cells grow quickly,

so they were innocent targets of the chemo.

I usually did the shots late at night, just before bed,

after trying to block out the idea all day long.

I endured the routine, though I never enjoyed it.

Most of the time Jeff would stay

to keep me company while I carefully set up.

First, I washed my hands with waterless antibacterial soap.

Next, I rubbed a sterile alcohol swab

on an unused piece of thigh and on the top of the vial.

Finally, I carefully aspirated the precious drug

into a sterile syringe.

Ten tiny vials cost $1200, so I didn't want to waste any.

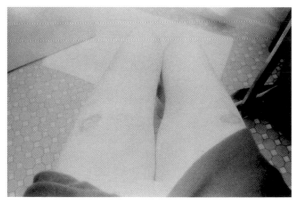

Shots : Head and Legs

Then came the hard part.

I had to pinch enough flesh so I could push the needle

up to the hilt into my thigh, and inject the drug.

I could have gone to a clinic or the hospital,

or had a nurse come in to give me the shots,

as many people do.

Learning how to do it myself

gave me a lot more autonomy about

when and where I would do my injections

and where I could go on a daily basis.

After I finished, I always covered

the needle hole with a happy, kids' Band-Aid

to mark the spot where I had last injected.

Jeff's Thoughts

Marcia has always been the tough patient.
The "no Novocain" type.
Never complains, but this was different.
No help from nurses, or Jeff.
She just wanted company.
I could handle that.
Amazing.

Becoming a Make-up Artist

This is just about as bald as you can get.

Without my eyelashes and eyebrows,

I became an experienced artist with an eyebrow pencil.

I attended an American Cancer Society

Look Good, Feel Better program.

In the past, as a volunteer for the ACS,

I had encouraged other women undergoing chemotherapy

to attend these sessions.

Now the session was for me.

As instructed, I washed my wigs once a week,

a pleasant change from my usual routine of daily lathers.

The two wigs were supposed to be identical

but I felt happier in one than the other

and wore it most of the time,

contrary to the orders of Edward.

Jeff's Thoughts
Wig on, wig off.
Is she Marcia, or Reid?
The chemo has affirmed her dual personality.

Bald in Black

The compliments on my new "haircut"

made me smile inwardly.

Fortunately, the wig survived the extra wear.

In a dream, I envisioned my favorite wig disintegrating,

leaving me with only the second choice.

I almost always wore my wig.

(Only a winter hat I loved didn't have room for the wig.)

To me, scarves screamed cancer.

I didn't want people feeling sorry for me,

averting their eyes, or staring.

A bare head was a challenge I didn't want to offer.

I could never bring myself to use

the double-faced tape

Edward gave me at the wig store.

If it was windy, I probably looked a little silly

not wearing a hat and holding my head.

To me that was better

than the sensation of Scotch tape

sticking to my skull.

Circlet

Compared to the Cat

Living a Normal Life

One winter morning I was sitting in the den reading.

I looked up at my cat, Chatchat,

who was resting in her favorite place,

the back of a chair in the sun.

Her hair looked so luxuriant.

I quickly snapped a photograph.

Trying to keep up a normal life

was important to me.

Staying fit was important, too —

mentally and physically.

I had been exercising religiously for ten years.

I started soon after recovery from my first cancer.

Once the new surgery scar had healed sufficiently,

I went back to my gym.

Jeff's Thoughts
Friends and family are (often, sometimes, usually)
there for you — Chatchat was always there for Marcia.
She was, and remains, a great source of comfort to Marcia.

I wasn't able to keep up with the aerobic and step classes,

so for the first time in my life I began working with a trainer.

I didn't want my muscles to atrophy.

I made a conscious effort to keep up with my art as well.

Sometimes I had to give myself a mental push.

It would have been easy to use illness

as an excuse to be a lump.

Taking the periodic self-portraits was one way

of continuing to be an artist.

I wrote artist grant and fellowship applications.

and entered art competitions, too.

I had some successes and some failures,

but I was used to that.

I had life on my mind.

That was my important focus.

I knew that letting everything go

would not be good for me.

I needed something to think about

besides my various doctor and hospital visits.

Life on My Mind

Time for Me

How did I cope? I followed the credo:

"Do something you've always wanted to do."

Something for myself. Something fun.

It could be as small as half an hour meditating

or as big as a trip to a place I'd always wanted to visit.

Then I'd go back to the routine, rejuvenated.

The daily responsibilities

of family life did not disappear

just because I had cancer.

And they shouldn't.

Taking some time for me was important.

I knew that attending to my needs at this time

was *not* selfish

and would help me maintain a sense of balance.

Jeff Remembers

The hair became the focus, not the cancer.
I think that helped us both.
Was her appearance strange?
Who cares? I didn't.

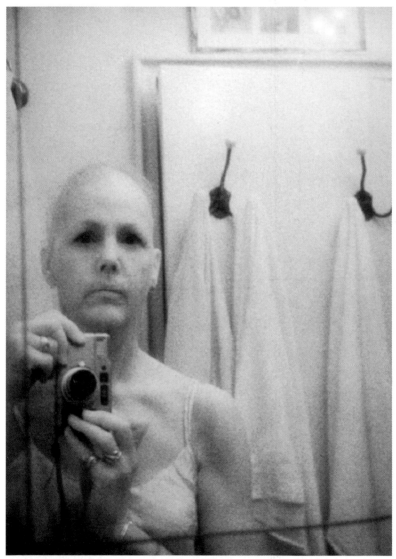

How Did I Cope ?

Mirroring

Transfusions

I had two transfusions.

Each time my red blood cell count

had dropped so low that climbing

a small set of stairs left me gasping.

I appreciated the blood donated by kind,

unknown souls who could still give blood

and would spend the time to do it.

As a cancer survivor I may feel good and healthy,

but my blood is not acceptable for donation.

I've had chemo — no blood from me.

I discovered this when I tried to give blood

after my first cancer.

Receiving blood is an energizing —

and life-giving — process

that takes about the same three or four hours

as a round of chemo.

While AIDS and hepatitis are not supposed to be

issues, the spectre is there, rational thought aside.

The Old Tree, Still Standing

Sex and More

Most doctors, I found,

seemed hesitant to talk about sexual matters.

My surgeon was an exception.

At my follow-up visit his first question was

"Have you tried sex yet?"

I was speechless. I had to admit that I hadn't.

I was afraid. I felt so fragile.

His encouragement made me realize that I was ready to try.

Jeff was pleased.

He hadn't wanted to push me.

A pleasant sexual encounter

helps to make you forget

some of the bad things

going on in your life.

With my other doctors, gynecologist included,

I had to be the one who wasn't embarrassed.

I had to bring it up.

It was worth the momentary intake of breath

I could see the doctor take,

to have my questions or concerns answered.

During treatment decisions for my first cancer,

I was amazed that the first radiologist I saw (a woman)

neglected to tell me that radiation therapy

would cause the death of my ovaries.

I had seen *seven* doctors

for various parts of my treatment

before my chosen radiologist (a man)

explained to me what the radiation would do.

I was more upset about this unexpected news

than about losing my colon.

Jeff's Thoughts
The more beautiful Marcia became
our physical relationship took an
unconscious time out.
For a while,
touching and kissing were
sustenance enough for us.

I Felt So Fragile

Out of the Doldrums

Some days I felt as though

I just wanted to sit around and do nothing.

I didn't allow that feeling to last long.

The worst thing, for me,

would be to let the cancer

or the treatment take over my life.

I would mentally pick myself up,

and physically go do something.

Work on my photography, go to the gym,

call one of my daughters,

drive into town to do a little shopping;

anything to keep my mind

and body from getting depressed.

My doctor called it denial.

Even today, I call it positive attitude.

I have never believed in the logic

in asking "Why me?"

or being angry at the unfairness of life.

Me with Many Lights

Why would I bother to focus

on an obviously unanswerable question,

wasting my time and energy?

Better to get on with the life I had

in the best way I could,

than to feel sorry for myself.

I tried, during my treatment,

to enjoy the world around me

— and I continue to do that.

Listen to new sounds, music, or the birds outside.

See the unusual, an art show, or a movie.

Smell the aromas around me,

the changes of the seasons, or supper cooking.

This attitude made my life easier

and, most likely,

the lives of those around me as well.

Jeff Remembers
— *So sick, but so strong.*
She just blanks out the pain,
the needles, the worries.

Around Me

After the Chemo

With the end of the chemo sessions,

my body was on its own.

My psyche was on its own.

It was a frightening feeling and a scary time.

(Memories of my first cancer came rushing back.)

When I was having chemotherapy,

there was all this unpleasant stuff going on —

but I knew the drugs must be at work.

The chemo was killing the cancer cells

and helping my body get rid of them.

Doctors and nurses watched over me.

I went for frequent office visits.

I was in contact with "things medical."

When I finished the course of chemo,

nothing was being done to fight the cancer.

Without vigilance, anything can happen.

I felt exactly the same eleven years ago

when I finished the treatments for my first cancer.

Pale Me, Close Up

Little Song

At the time, I thought there should be a special
"End-of-Chemo" visit for patients when it was time
to space the follow-up appointments further apart.

I had created a version of my idea for my doctor.
It included reminders about follow-up visits
and periodic tests that would be necessary.
The form waited silently in my computer
for someone to recognize the need for it.

Ten years later, I felt that same unease
when the chemo was finished.
I mentioned my concerns, and my form,
to my homeopathic doctor
and she asked me if she could see it.
She thought her patients might find it useful.
Perhaps it is finally helping someone.*

Jeff's Input
Must be a strange period
for all involved in cancer treatment.
Anti-climactic is not quite the feeling.
Everyone wonders — now what happens?

(* See Appendix, pg. 122: "End-of-Chemo Form.")

The Journey Begins

Here, with *The Swing* as the centerpiece,

began the journey to my book.

In May, to celebrate the end of my chemo,

I went to Santa Fe to attend a workshop called

A Gathering of Women Photographers.

The workshop was as much about

finding yourself as a person

as it was about photography.

The Swing was a symbol of the workshop.

We often gathered there as a group

or found a moment for solitary meditation.

Each day we would do exercises

aimed at encouraging trust and caring.

Jeff's Thoughts

I loved the picture of the swing when I first saw it,

but it made me sad

to confront what it meant to me.

The Swing

One activity involved half the group lying

on the floor, eyes closed,

while the other half

chose a partner from the prone group.

Each partner would, then, sit down behind her choice

and, without speaking, gently lift her head.

During my turn to have my head lifted,

all I could think of was my wig.

Would it fall off, exposing me?

I realized I was not getting,

or giving,

the full benefit of the exercise.

I hadn't planned to show my bare head.

Once again, as I had reacted during my treatment,

I didn't want people feeling sorry for me.

I didn't want them to think

I was looking for sympathy.

Here it was different,

I realized.

At the next opportunity

to discuss a life situation with the group,

I knew I would have to tell the story

of my feelings during the exercise,

and remove my wig.

Admitting the truth

at the session that evening

allowed me to become

fully involved in the course.

The other women

appreciated my honesty.

Their heartfelt prayers

gave me encouragement

to be more open with them

and with myself as well.

Going Wigless

One day in June,

after I had come home from the workshop,

I was headed for an aerobics class at the gym.

It was a boiling hot day.

I thought, "If I could go wigless in New Mexico,

why not try wigless in Connecticut."

I walked in and took what had been my usual place,

on the right near the windows, in the back row.

No one said hello. No one looked at me.

No one glanced in my direction, even in the mirror.

I felt invisible.

It seemed they wanted me to be invisible.

I realized that in the wider world,

even the gym where attitudes might be more accepting,

a bald head was too much of a statement for me to make.

(Maybe not too much for somebody else,

but certainly for me.)

So that was the end of that experiment.

Prickly

My Dolls, Ready for a Shoot

Ready for a Shoot

I often photographed these dolls

to use as baby cards

for the birth of friends' grandchildren.

They were set up for a photo.

Looking at them, I had a hair revelation.

The bald baby doll

belonged to my mother when she was a child.

Now I was bald like the baby.

The shape of my head was exposed, like hers.

The Teddy bear

was my source of courage when I was four.

The Italian doll with the bountiful hair

was a reminder

of what I could look like

when all this was finished.

Jeff's Thoughts
The doll photographs were
an independent project that became,
by design or happenstance,
dramatically symbolic.

The Wig I Wore

The Wig Versus Baldness

This is me in my favorite wig.

I felt comfortable with it on.

I think I looked quite normal, too.

At night I didn't wear the wig.

When it was cold, I often wore a little cap

I'd ordered from the American Cancer Society's

catalogue of wigs and accoutrements.*

I could hardly believe it. Jeff *liked* my bald head.

He asked for a portrait of me, wigless.

I had it taken for him by Joyce Tenneson,**

co-founder of the *Gathering* workshop.

He thinks it is wonderful.

Joyce included it in her recent book, *Light Warriors.*

I'm happy to remember me with hair.

Jeff Remembers
The wig was okay,
to avoid questions and comments.
Without it she was starkly beautiful.

(* See Appendix, pg. 120: "Night Cap," **"Joyce.")

There's a Shadow

It Will Return

This is me with a tiny shadow

of potential hair.

I could see that contrary to my fears,

my hair was going to grow back.

I wasn't going to be bald forever.

It seemed such a long wait.

The last vestiges of hair disappeared

in early January,

and the last chemo was on April 27.

The first appearance

of a new fuzz of hair wasn't until July.

Jeff Speaks
Wow.
There it is.
Sure took a long time.

Family Time

It was important for me to have

family and friends around.

I knew they needed to see that

I could feel well.

It was a comfort to me to have them there

to be able to help if I was feeling down.

My family wanted to be a part

of my life and my illness.

We valued time spent together.

Precious moments became poignant ones.

Light on the Pool

Good-Bye to the Wig

I was trying to capture on film

the growing corona

of new hair I could see

 — and feel.

The last time I wore my wig

was in August, at a wedding.

I had about a quarter of an inch of hair.

I've hardly ever had short hair.

This "cut" looked very fashionable

to the unknowing eye,

but I didn't want to make a statement

at someone else's wedding,

so I wore the wig.

The next week we went on vacation.

My wig stayed home.

The biggest hair problem

I encountered on the trip

was a chilly head.

Hair Halo, Back-Lighted

What Does the Future Hold? What Do I Do About It?

There are questions and wondering

and worries floating in my head.

Lots of trying to think positively.

What is that ache in my back?

A bone metastasis

or just too much activity over the weekend?

I must remember, I am getting older.

An acquaintance develops cancer

and calls asking for suggestions.

I must remember to be positive.

Forget that bad headache the other day.

It is not a brain metastasis.

Be helpful.

A friend dies of cancer.

For a few days I feel both guilty and lucky that I am not

the one who dies, that I am still alive.

"Life guilt" I call it.

I don't know if others feel it, too. I don't ask.

The Black Crow

I never skip the follow-up visits.

Check-ups are scheduled every three months.

Later they will be spaced

further and further apart.

The days right before a visit are difficult.

Each twinge portends evil metastatic cells.

Then the CT scan, the blood test,

the visit — are past.

There is nothing visible.

I go on about my business.

These tests

and days of tension,

have been a part of my life

since my first cancer —

and they don't go away.

Into the Picture

Will I Return to Normal?

I look healthy to the casual observer.

And I am. Only I know my new limitations.

I can't do aerobics the way I used to —

two classes in a row.

Now I feel lucky to struggle

through forty-five minutes,

doing mostly low impact.

I can't bounce down a set of stairs

the way I used to.

I can't walk up a set of stairs

without getting somewhat breathless.

Still, I always drag myself up four or five flights,

rather than take the elevator.

Jeff Speaks
She is getting better (I hope)
but this is not my Marcia.
I want the Marcia I remember.
I love you.
I am crying.

Color Coming Back

I always walk rather than ride,

and that includes escalators.

Exercise has been an integral part of my life

during the ten years since my last cancer.

It's a state of mind I work to maintain.

I haven't lost that need

to sweat and feel tired

and know that I am healthier for it.

I continue to focus on staying fit

because I feel better when I exercise;

both my physical self and my self-esteem benefit.

For me being active functions, just as the articles say,

as a natural anti-depressant.

I notice a difference if I miss a few days.

The need to exercise pulls at me.

I can see and feel my progress

and value the effort it takes to become stronger.

The Chapel Wall

My List of Preventive Measures — for Me —
and for Other Cancer Patients to Think About

I stay vigilant.

I do not skip the follow-up visits

with my oncologist or other doctors.

I didn't let the gynecologist tell me

"it's just radiation damage" and turn away.

I wouldn't let any doctor do that.

I consider any strange feelings

that continue longer than two or three weeks

to be possible recurrent cancer.

I talk about them with my oncologist.

If I don't feel right,

I don't put it off.

I ACT.

I try to listen to my body.

Preventive Measures for the Healthy

If you do not have cancer and you are reading this book,

below are some hints I have gathered for you.

Follow the preventive highway.

If a screening test is due, have it.

If it isn't a fun test — like the infamous colonoscopy,

give yourself a prize after you have been through it —

but have the dreaded test.

If you don't feel right — go to a doctor.

If your doctor says you are OK

and you still don't feel right — go to another doctor.

Don't let anyone tell you what you *know*

about your own body is wrong.

Learn the seven cancer warning signs

(unusual bleeding, in my case) and watch for them.

The sooner you find a cancer,

the better off you will be,

so don't blind yourself to its possibility.

(* See Appendix: pg. 121 "Cancer's Seven ...")

Many Me's

About My Hair — One Year Later

Here I am with hair that has grown

long enough to cut a couple of times

to keep it in shape.

It hasn't been dyed.

I decided to give that up.

Now is a time to avoid unnecessary poisons.

I look like a Karakul lamb.

My mother used to have a lambskin coat

that had almost the same colors and texture,

a curly mixture of gray and brown.

When I was a child I had ringlets.

Later I had waves.

The chemo left me with tight curls.

I've been asked where I got my perm.

A friend had chemo similar to mine.

Her hair grew in as straight as a stick.

An acquaintance who had chemotherapy

told me her hair grew in extremely curly.

Now, a year later,

her hair is quite straight.

I'll just have to wait to discover

what will happen to me and my hair.

I try not to become too enamored

with what I have now.

Lighting Up

Together, New Year's Eve,

Here we are.

New Year's Eve of the Millennium,

relaxed and contented on this historic night.

Nineteen-ninety-nine was a year to remember,

and to forget.

It was the perfect time to start on a new life.

We are still together.

Jeff has been patient with my ups and downs

and continues to be.

Writing this book has been therapeutic.

The work helped me maintain my positive attitude

and has pushed me to places

I surely would not otherwise have gone.

I hope that those of you who read it

will find encouragement in it.

The Two of Us

Me in Color

Back to a Life

Back to a life that is as normal as any life.

January, 2000

Jeff's Final Thoughts.

Marcia and her hair have changed.

So have I.

Time for us to move on.

My Web Site:
www.aboutmyhair.net
has a number of useful links.

* Notes for Page 26   **Information about Wigs**:

My wigs came from: **Bitz-and-Pieces**,
226 Columbus Ave. NYC 10023
which can be reached at 1-**212-787-3941.**

On the Internet, the computer literate might also try accessing
the following websites:

http://npntserver.mcg.edu/html/alopecia/AlopeciaFAQ(part05).html
for a discussion on baldness (with a leaning towards the disease
alopecia, which means hair loss, and results in baldness similar
to the baldness that affects people on chemotherapy).
It has an excellent discussion on wigs and lists of places to buy wigs.

The following are some suggestions from the Alopecia site:

http://www.WIGEXPRESS.COM/
http://www.sheitel.com or search for Hana's Wigs

http://www.worldofwigs.com has a special section related to chemo.
http://www.continentalhair.com/ is a website from Canada that has a
lot of information about wigs and provides details about the different
types of hair used to make human hair wigs.
http://www.wigoutlet.com

http://www.headcovers.com. Just what the name says, headcovers
(i.e., turbans and hats, as well as wigs) made for alopecians.
http://www.cheryn.com.

* Notes for Page 46

Alternative Therapies
   In General:
http://dailynews.yahoo.com/fc/Health/Alternative_Medicine
   Specific:
Acupuncture: http://www.demon.co.uk/acupuncture/
Reiki: Tera Mai Reiki — **http://teramaireiki.tripod.com/**
presents the history of Reiki and how it works
Rosen Method: A gentle massage/talk therapy session
is extremely calming. There are two main sites :
http://www.rosenmethod.org//
http://www.rosenmethod.com/

* Notes for Page 93

Night Cap
from TLC *(Tender Loving Care)* Catalogue
Phone: 800.850.9445 for a copy or to order.
The website **(www.tlccatalogue.org)** can be reached
through the general American Cancer Society site:
http://www.cancer.org
or for more information you can write:
American Cancer Society
National Home Office
1599 Clifton Road NE
Atlanta, GA 30329-4115

or visit your local ACS chapter.

** Additional Notes for Page 93,

Joyce
Light Warriors, by Joyce Tenneson. 2000, Bullfinch Press.
ISBN 0-8212-2698-3.

* Notes for Page 109

Cancer's Seven Warning Signs from Oncolink:
http://cancer.med.upenn.edu/causeprevent/screening/tip1016.html

> A Change in bowel or bladder habits
> A sore that does not heal
> Unusual bleeding or discharge
> Thickening or lump in breast or elsewhere
> Indigestion or difficulty in swallowing
> Obvious change in wart or mole
> Nagging cough or hoarseness.

Another warning sign, not listed by the ACS, but one to watch is:
any unexplained weight loss.

For more information, you can also visit:

The American Cancer Society website: **www.cancer.org**
or

Oncolink at the University of Pennsylvania:
http://cancer.med.upenn.edu
also

many other websites from Cancer Centers all over the United States.

For Survivorship Issues visit the ACS's Cancer Survivors Network,
at **www.acscsn.org**
There are stories by cancer survivors, categorized by age, sex and
type of cancer. There are also web pages and images placed on the site
by cancer survivors.

* Exit Interview Form from Page 83

Physicians' Offices
Helen & Harry Gray Cancer Center
Hartford Hospital
Hartford, Connecticut 06125
Date: /   /

End-of-treatment Interview for _____
(Patient's name)

With: Dr. _____
(Doctor's name)

Now that you have finished your chemotherapy, we will no longer be seeing you as frequently as we have been.   You may find that you continue to feel tired and have symptoms similar to those that occurred during treatment. Do not be alarmed. This is normal for up to 4-6 weeks after your treatment stops.

We will want to see you in 6 weeks for a thorough post-treatment check-up. After that appointment, we will want you to come back to see us at _____ month intervals for the next year.

Your first follow-up appointment will be on: _____ at _____.

Your appointment will include one or more of the following tests (circled) :

Complete physical exam	Ultrasound	MRI	CT Scan
Liver Scan	Bone Scan	Mammogram	
Chest X-ray	Barium enema	CBC (Complete Blood Count)	
CEA	CA125	Creatinine	Billirubin
Stool tests - for blood	Colonoscopy	Other: _____	

Your Physician's Assistant/Nurse will be: ._____
Feel free to call her/him at: Phone #_____
Other Notes/Comments:

You should also call Dr. _____ for an appointment in _____..

If you have any questions or concerns between visits,
please don't hesitate to call us.

We are happy that your treatment is finished,
but we will still be here if you need us.

Watching and Waiting

Acknowledgments

Without my concerned, caring and efficient doctors, especially
Jeff Cohen and Pat DeFusco, there might not be a me to write
this.
I thank them with all my heart.

The *Gathering of Women Photographers* sent me on this journey.
Their initial positive reactions to my photographs at the
workshop in Santa Fe were the genesis of my book. The
members of the *Gathering* continue to support and encourage me.

They deserve special mention:
Joyce Tenneson and Elise Wiarda were the leaders. Members
included: Susan Burgess, Marge Casey, Joyce Chadwick, Greta
Easdon, Sheila Fagan, Ginny Felch, Susan Ferris, Jane Gleeson,
Sheila Goode, Carol Granger, Renie Haiduk, Clair Kipness, Jill
Kokesh, Melissa Ladd, Marla McDonald, Melissa Powledge, and
Leith Rohr.

My dear husband, Jeff, had no idea what he was getting into
when he married me. I love him for standing by me and with
me through the long journey and onward.

My daughters, Melissa and Amanda, and their husbands cared
for me and about me, and even now make sure I take care of
myself. I hope they know how much I love them.

I couldn't have put the book together without Michael Zych,
my photographic assistant, who is also editor, critic, web
designer, and sounding board.

Many people read various stages of this Journal and offered
critiques, editing and other suggestions. The list became too long
to print. To each of you: I thank you. I found your help
invaluable and appreciate the time you all gave to my project.

Regina Barreca supported my work and used her own writing
to get my story out. Kathleen Spivack is my writing consultant.
Her expertise and encouragement sent me to the next level.
She made me make the small changes that counted so much.
Peter White, who never lost patience with me, was much more
than "the printer." His graphic design suggestions gave the
book exactly the professional touches it needed.

Nancy Grover was emotionally and intellectually supportive.
Many years of friendship and our shared experiences with
chemotherapy have created a strong bond.

A special friend, Alison Gill, is someone who would have helped
me, but couldn't – her cancer was ovarian.

Andy Salner believed in my project from the beginning
and in his calm, quiet way, helped to make it happen.

Love to all of you.

What Others Say About *About My Hair*

Andrew Salner, Director, Helen & Harry Gray Cancer Center, Hartford Hospital, and Radiation Oncologist. This poignant written and photo diary beautifully documents Marcia's journey through her cancer diagnosis and treatment and demonstrates the supports which have helped her cope with her illness and therapy and maintain her positive outlook. For those patients and families concerned about the impact of cancer therapy, her book serves as an inspiration related to the strength of the human spirit. It also demystifies some of the side effects of treatment and at the same time provides hope for the future. Her powerful photos and story provide inspiration for all of us as we deal with the challenges in our lives.

Patricia DeFusco, My Oncologist. To triumph over cancer not once but twice requires stamina, humor, grace and perseverance. To understand and interpret the experience for others requires insight, honesty and perspective. Marcia Marsted not only exemplifies these qualities, but has been able to use her unique talents to provide us with this wonderful chronicle of her experience. Her diary helps us all to step back and understand the human dimension of this process that we call cancer. By so doing, this diary reminds us to be more compassionate, more attentive and aware of the importance that even small issues have to our patients.

Molly Punzo, MD, Doctor of Homeopathy, and Director of Integrative Medicine at Hartford Hospital. Marcia's book is a dauntingly honest and courageous visual portrayal of one person's healing journey through cancer and out the other side. A visual narrative of transformation. Her artistic expression is deeply moving, profoundly brave, and humanely authentic.

Nancy Grover, Friend and Fellow Cancer Survivor. Marcia's Journal is a profile in courage, resilience, and hope for all who battle this disease. Her remarkable journey will be a meaningful and inspiring guide for her fellow travelers.

Bijay Mukherji, Professor of Medicine, University of Connecticut Health Center. This is a poetic tale of a "journey" through life, cruelly punctuated by the ravages of a second cancer, yet made admirably bearable by the unshakable will to overcome adversity and with enduring love – two primal elements that sustain life itself.

Steven Lowy, Artist, Curator and Consciousness Teacher. I believe your book is important because not every doctor is a healer. The psychological, homeopathic and other modalities you explored to maintain your health are unknown to the greater part of humanity.

Jill Ciment, Marcia's Personal Trainer, Aerobic and Yoga Instructor. ...her red blood cell count...was low, to the point that I knew a workout would probably only make her more fatigued - then I understood - it wasn't so much about the workout itself as it was about just working out. That feeling of accomplishment when it's over....My one regret - not knowing to acknowledge Marcia the day she walked into class wigless. I thought pointing her out ...would have made her uncomfortable. I was wrong. She was never invisible in our eyes.

Marilyn Sheinberg, Marcia's Hairstylist. I have been Marcia's hairstylist for over twenty years, and I am proud to say that I regard her more as a dear friend than a client. Before her hair loss, we avoided a drastic change in her appearance by deciding to cut her hair short and styling her wigs to match. Seeing her hair grow back better than before was a thrill and a joy for me. Marcia's inner strength and incredible zest for life make her an amazing woman.

About My Hair :
A Journey to Recovery

by **Marcia Reid Marsted**

The book is available through amazon.com
or directly from the publisher:

Capelli d'Angeli Press
125 Indian Hill Road
Canton, CT 06019

www.capellidangelipress.net

Each Book: *About My Hair :*
                   A Journey to Recovery $15.00

Shipping/Handling $ 5.00
Total $20.00

To Order   Send a check or money order payable to
                Capelli d'Angeli Press to the above address.
                Include your name, address, zip code
                and phone number.

                Email: capellidangelipress@yahoo.com
                if you have questions or comments

The book sells for $15.00 plus $5.00 shipping and handling.

I plan to donate a portion of the selling price to the wonderful
hospitals and charitable organizations that help cancer patients.

If you would like to send more, I will donate it.